# VINCULUM

# VINCULUM

poems

Alice Friman

Louisiana State University Press
Baton Rouge

Published by Louisiana State University Press
Copyright © 2011 by Alice Friman
All rights reserved
Manufactured in the United States of America
LSU Press Paperback Original
First printing

DESIGNER: Michelle A. Neustrom
TYPEFACE: Tribute
PRINTER AND BINDER: IBT Global

LIBRARY OF CONGRESS CATALOGING-IN-PUBLICATION DATA

Friman, Alice.
  Vinculum : poems / Alice Friman.
    p. cm.
  "LSU Press Paperback Original."
  Includes bibliographical references.
  ISBN 978-0-8071-3787-1 (pbk. : alk. paper)
  I. Title.
  PS3556.R5685V56 2011
  811'.54—dc22

                    2010038068

To Rich and Julie, Paul and Jackie, Lillian and John

and, as ever, to Bruce

# CONTENTS

# VINCULUM

# Seeing It Through

Presto the magician
drops his handkerchief
and amazingly I'm looking down
seventy years. Down
as from the top of a winding stair
vertigoing to the bottom
where the child struggles to mount
crawling on her knees that first step.
And I want to say Wait
I'll come down
carry you up
for I need you here
now that the banister is nearing
its finial and I can see
the rituals of the sky
speeding up through the almost
reachable skylight.

Honey hair and the sunsuit
Mother made from a scrap. Come.
If I hold you high, you can touch
the glass. Let the last contact
be a baby's hand. Why not?
All things come around
replete with rage and rattle.

I

# The Black Tupelo

Behind the veil of branches
that swirl to the ground,
the naked trunk of the dance—
*Nyssa sylvatica,* named for the nymphs
who nursed Dionysus after he was
twice born and for whom he's named.
And maybe in Nyssa, "loveliest of valleys"
beyond the known world, they danced
to distract a tantrum or hush a whimper,
indulging his whim to swipe at the ribbons
flying from their shoulders
in a contagion of laughter, for he was god.

The Latin name is all that's left
of that old story. But when I part
the falling fountain of these branches,
I enter as through a beaded curtain
the room of the forbidden—
the sacred cave of air that trembles around
nakedness and the wine glass of the body
caught in a gesture of profound grace.
Here is the holy place of childhood, here
under the hair of trees. You remember—
the neighbor boy, the lovely giggles. You.

## *Ars Poetica* in Green

I walk a woods deep as Dante's Error.
A path, abandoned by sun, green as toad
in the shade of the mandrake. A tunnel
of green time. I, the only traveler.

The colors of spring—violet, bluets,
pinks—gone now, except by the muddy ditch
where sun pokes in to pet his favorite
flies, and gangs of purple clover, girlgangs
tough as nails painted Revlon's Mauve Mystique,
make kissy lips  X  X  and slap my shoe
while a congregation of butterflies—
hypocrites all—gather on clods of dirt
to clap their stained-glass wings.
                              Then once more, trees
roar up to close above my head and I
am dropped again in green. A cylinder
fallen on its side to walk through. A time
half past no time, tonic and tinted air.
Verdi's aria in G. Serenade
in chlorophyll. Woo room, green vagina,
tube of love. And there, in the dim cloister
of these woods, two identical beetles
stuck together like cars with locked bumpers.
Not VW Bugs as you might think
but 1952 Buicks shining
in metallic emerald, plugged-in green.
And despite my fame and behemoth shoes,
they do not move, screwed to the sticking place,
as if one rear-ended the other in
this lovers' lane where every day, all day,
a green light says Go Go Go. So they stayed.

I scuff my sneakers, click my tongue, yet still
they stick, immovable. The film jamming
to a halt as if the golden sprockets
of this world having had enough, bit down,
gnashing their teeth to stop it. To show, here
on this path, how two mere bugs can provide
all brightness necessary. Oh, Lady—
never to shrivel in your emerald skin,
weep or shiver, covered as you are by
the green hardtop of his body. And You—
gripping perfection at last, never to
let go. Your tiny mandible kisses
sacred now as Masaccio's Peter
standing still as paint on a wall, to heal
the leper with his shadow. The exact
moment caught and trembling above the brim
even of consequences, boiled down and
frozen, so we can carry for a while
a whole world's weight or wish hammered into
gesture like Keats's marathon of swains
hot-footing it around an urn, playing
puckerlips, forever stiff in Wedgwood.

Even in *our* time, if you remember—
Redford to Streep in *Out of Africa*
when under the four-poster canopy
of her bed in the pulled shade of love's green
afternoon, boiling sheets, and she stuffed with
his gorgeousness: "Don't move," he said. "Don't move."

# Cascade Falls

LIEBER STATE PARK, INDIANA

Every man I ever wanted
I brought here for a picnic. Walked him out

over these horizontal slabs to swish
our feet in the water. Packed lunch,

my breasts for dessert. I always drove.
It was a surprise, you see. But you

I never brought. Let's face it, you began
as understudy. I had to prompt your lines.

This was big time. Standing Room Only
(those jostling trees). And O, the acting,

the Stanislavski method working that green O.
The besotted cliffs echoing with praise. Don't

feel bad. By the time you fumbled on the scene
the scene was Greek, and I, burning to bury

not *two* brothers but a regiment. I was Jocasta
stabbed with dress pins, Medea drenched in blood

not wet enough to wash the anger from my hands,
and Agamemnon's wife, so picnicked out, so wax-

papered in duplicity, I was without shame.
No, I never brought you here, even now,

for what if time's membrane did not hold
and the double axe of Clytemnestra's words

crashed through my teeth, and Jason
snarled again in your voice? What of

Aristotle's unities, not to mention our own,
for how many years of marriage shored up

is dike enough, dead-bolt and chain enough
when such tempting lines are practiced

and cued up on an unsuspecting tongue?

# The Price

We were a process
going nowhere, fueled
on poetry and any old thing
to eat. Even in the bathtub, be-
tween slosh and fondle, we were Rich
and Sexton, Hass and *listen to this.*
Oh, but weren't we lovely then?
You were my delirium, my
silver ring, my Mercury, all lithe-
limbed stream and glitter. And I,
young again and too much in love
to be turned into your boulder—
the mote in your eye.

Today, twenty-five years later,
the trees outside my window
once again dandle their darlings,
tossing in the blue air spring's
green adorables, knowing
full well the coming sacrifice,
the shriveling end. And I wonder
if when these trees are gone,
the future will be able to read
the invisible ink ground into
their pulp, pressed into their paper,
saying After, there was blank.
Then there was inconsolable.

## Visiting the Territories

Come, brush the clay
from what's left of your good suit
and lie down here with me.
                              In the splinters
of what you are, in the marrow's residue,
surely there are traces of your bride.
Don't be afraid. Make believe I'm asking
you to dance. You always loved to dance.
*Show 'em how it's done in Brooklyn,* you'd say,
whirling me out to the ends of your fingers,
pulling me back.
                              Now I'm pulling you
back, not to redraw the lines or rummage
in the ragbag of our *forever after,*
but because I need you. Come.
Our first apartment, a high-rise called
The Dakota, remember? A big joke
for two New York City big shots like us
who couldn't find the Dakotas on a map
if we had to. Birdland, that we knew, Basie,
Embers East, Oscar Peterson, and Dinah un-
dressing the blues in pink. Dizzy, healing
the world with his horn, holding the whole
damn ball in his cheeks. Who'd not reconvene
his dust to remember that?
                              Come. Apt. 4-C.
Five-and-ten-store dishes and all we own—
a mattress, Scrabble, and a window fan
rattling its dark inklings. Maybe if you lay
down next to me the artless bones, I could find
the true history of the Dakotas before the broken
treaties, the Badlands, and what happened next.

# Siren Song for Late September

A woman walks the trails at night
wondering where the insects are,
and why this forest, second in dampness
to the Great Northwest, lets them out
only in daylight.
               She hears them though,
chirr-chirring in their leafy chains—
slaves to the galley drum of summer
straining for one last wave of heat.

Who doesn't know, given the stuff
of dreams, what pitch black unleashes?
How, when her flashlight dies, that sound
will conspire with the rustling walls
to close in, mocking her terror.
                    Even
the path her shoes have memorized,
the sweet meander back to the lamp
and unfinished letter on the table, yields.

Like the newly blind, feeling along
a long corridor, what stingy choice
does she have, betrayed on such a cold
and moonless night by the very ground
beneath her feet,
               but to hold out her hands
to the singing walls, the leg-rubbing, leaf-
cutting walls, smelling of sinkhole and rot.
Black-veined gloves reaching to touch her.

## Depression Glass

It must have been October, right after
the annual hanging of the winter drapes
and the ceremonial unrolling of the rug
from its summer sleep behind the sofa.
Gone were the slipcovers, leaving
the upholstery stripped down to warm
arms again, and the little living room
transformed into a mother hug of all
she labored for—the luxury of bastion
and snug, the thick stability of thick
pile, purchased with how many
on-her-knees hours of scour and rag.
The whir of the sewing machine at night,
and all those stretched nickels.

*My sister would say this never happened,*
*or if it did, it wasn't this way, or if it was,*
*I never cried, or if I did, how could I—*
*so young—know what was to cry about.*

A room like that, in the Snow White
haven of the dwarves' house, and I
no more than four, rowing a cardboard
box across the rug, its flowered sea
lapping at my hands that were my oars.
When suddenly, there was my father
dancing to the radio or some crazy song
of his own making, flapping his arms
and yawping like a great enchanted
gull of happiness having nothing to do
with me. Or her. And I saw as through
the glass layers of the sea what he'd
been before I came in my little boat

grinding its vast engines of responsibility,
dragging him under, changing him into
someone other than the drowned beloved
I'd be trying to make it up to all my life.

# Waiting

Life isn't long enough
to learn the patience necessary.
Pitted against desire, what's so hot about
counting to ten? Think salmon—the fight,
the desperate fling
                              against the bear's
swipe and the knock-you-back water.
In the face of need, let's face it,
patience is luxury. Even Beauty,
sensible, yes, but come first thaw
she too is cruising for the hook.
No lure, no worm, no hand-tied fly
but whooped up already, ready to thrash
gasping in the bilge of any boat.
                              One ogle,
one polished line, one invitation into
the tangoed dark, and there it is—the red
slam-dunk of the heart, that timpani
in the chest counting out
the clarinet's twiddle and each thin
thought of the violin, wanting only
the great drama it was tightened up for.
The big BIM BAM.
                              Listen, the heart
wants what it wants. There's no telling
it different. Look out the window.
The curtain rises, and stage left—see?
Spring enters singing forsythia, that aria
of yellow, that operatic bush.

# Watching You in the Mirror

Suppose I stood behind you,
slipped my bare arms under yours
and arced them about, making you
into a four-armed god, all ministering
to your fresh-from-the-shower nakedness—
combing, deodorizing, touching
toothpaste to your brush—while you
concentrated on shaving, twisting
your mouth in that funny way you do.

Would you, compelled
by the light streaming in the window,
lift up one foot as if to dance—toes flexed,
heel down—and balancing on one leg,
glow as Shiva did in that ring of fire?

And if I suddenly bit you
the way I do sometimes, and you
unable to turn, caught in the bas-
relief of the game, how would you
read me? I have played wife
so well for fifteen years. Turban-
wrapped behind you, my name, Surya,
copper-headed daughter of the sun
who, like my father roaring in the ether,
loves to linger over skin, using her teeth
to know you. The gods say death comes only
to those who blink. Gods never blink
or shut their eyes, but shuffle the world,
growing tusks long with knowledge.

Husband, I tell you, there will be no end
to my knowing. In the reflection of my eyes,

you shall never sleep. If necessary, I will
gnaw each mirror you're in, swallowing
it down to keep you awake and inside me.

# Imitating Nature

Let us shed and then to bed
now that we've walked the woods
in November's fading light, the day's
dream sliding down without a cloud
for cover. The trees
stripped to the plain girls they are,
blemished and vulnerable. The world
having had enough of gorgeousness.

Let me introduce my parts. These
are my *Purities*. The right one, *Rosebud.*
The one over my heart, *The Egyptian,*
for unlike her sister she is heavy-veined
and serious, recalling how in ancient Thebes
the rivers of the breast were painted blue.
That's true. They say even in the dark
Antony could trace them to their source,
and when in Rome, plotting or reaching
for a grape, he was lost, drowned
in the fountain of those tributaries.

And here is my belly, this talcumed
absence of muscle, this stretch of sky
soft as a buttoned cushion. Today
her name shall be *Heaven*. Don't laugh.
A woman's prerogative: evening star,
morning star, Venus changes names
by the hour, and trees rename themselves
with each new dress. Why not the body?

Her name is *Heaven*. And see—
scattered across like lucky stars, seven
dancing petechiae, stigmata of ruby slippers—

*The Pleiades.* The seven daughters
of Atlas. My corundums. My red jewels.

This one I call *Justice,* that one
*Flair,* and my favorite—*Capital A*
for alpha, for apple, for Alice, for
Akbar the Great, ruler of the ruby throne.
And here, a childhood freckle. *Lioness*
because she prowls at night on the other side
of the scar that runs the length of me
like a junkyard fence. And there
where you've tucked your hand, there—
that's no petechia, no ruby among rubies.
That's *Folly,* the little lady herself,
still sashaying onto the dance floor
each time the band strikes up, carrying
nothing but a parasol and a little red purse.

II

# Silent Movie

One afternoon of rain and suddenly
creeks rise, babbling in the forest—
back-up singers for the silence.
A missed cue. It's November now,
the trees, bare. A light piano of chirp
and scurry is more than enough. Trees
make eloquent speech just by how
they stand or lean in graceful habit.
Or in the case of the sycamore, gleam
like polished marble in the sun.

The towering beech, the naked poplar
speak the language of lips and the moss
that covers them. If the trees sleep now
in this storage locker of the cold,
if they seem aloof and alien strange,
it doesn't mean that beneath the bark,
or underground where roots tangle
and hold, they've forgotten their promise
of smolder and juice. Look at them.
Valentino looked like that—waiting, still.

## Autobiography: The Short Version

I was born under the sign of Libra: up
down, teetering for balance: a spider,
all scurry and retreat, or the brass lamp
lighting up a room.

What I wanted was fulcrum—
the point of the knife: danger and no sleep.
What I got was desire, hard edged,
gleaming and perfect.

For that I was never forgiven.

I shouted huge, terrorized each day
with a violent fondle to make it give,
imitated the anteater tonguing sweetness up—
or the bear, honeycomb for the taking.

Learning to lie like that . . . that came later.

How to count your days as more
than cracks in a sidewalk. How to say
*No, not for a moment* to crackers and milk
or the hand-me-down life. How to not
see yourself taped up in the lobster tank—claws
and clappers scraping a slow motion against glass.

How else are we supposed to live,
seeing the boulders in the field sporting
their blue brooches of lichen or the cold night sky
tipsy in sequins and runaway fire?

# Vinculum

FOR RICHARD

Do not look at me again like that: between us
is too stripped down to the bare wire of what we were.

The look, umbilical—that cord I thought discarded
in some hospital bin fifty years ago come November.

How strange to find it once more between us,
still beating and so palpable we could

cross over and enter into each other again,
seeing our old selves through new, first eyes.

Plucked from a drumroll of autumns, that one
was ours—autumn of my twenty-third year, autumn

of your final fattening, taking up all the room,
worrying the thinning walls. The rope that seethed

from me to you and back again—our two-
way street—and you, little fish, hanging on

past your lease in a time of narrowing dark,
which you can't possibly remember, but do.

And it comes to me: that look must be what *love* is,
which is why we'll not speak of it nor hunt it down

in each other's eyes again, for you're too worldly
to admit, without wincing, what happened happened.

And I, too conscious of my failed attempts
to fire into language what's beyond words, could not

bear it. Which leaves me holding the bag once more
of foolish thoughts. I know, I know, the universe

has neither edge nor center nor crown, but I want
to think that past Andromeda and out beyond

a million swirling disks of unnamed stars, that cord
we knew, that ghost of an eye-beam floating between us,

arcs in space, lit up like the George Washington Bridge
pulsing with traffic, even after both stanchions are gone.

# Wind

Red-tagged around the middle,
four diagonal trees.
Dead men walking. Blood
on the lintel. The red decree
of who's next.

When I was seven I was sure
if I waved my arms
hard enough, if I ran
with the wind urging me,
pressing at my back,
I could fly.

For all I know
the wind only wanted to touch me.
Lovingly. The way all summer
it pets the leaves
forever quivering
and whispering about it
among themselves.

## Permanent Press

When I think of that summer, it opens
like a pleat in cloth: lake, tree, out-
blooming itself. What deep delicious
yardage of suffering: the virginal
July we defended, all the while itching
willful and goatish. Five hundred larks
rising from the fields and all I could do
was stare at the scar on your arm—
the gold embroidery I longed to touch.

What difference that time and pharmacology
delivered too late? I loved you then
in the old way of longing. Four wars,
nine recessions, ten presidents: patches.
Each year another July flings her ribboned
hat into the ring, another summer trying to
duplicate ours. Who were we on that park
bench that defies being folded and put away?
Forget it. Are you still alive? The rest is gibberish.

# Geometry

Mono-buttocked in a girdle,
& brassiered into cones—their satin
sister act pointy under wraps—we were
more than Euclidian globes & conicals
or the buzzy triangle we struggled
not to think about. If we were
two-faced & all angles toward
matrimony as we were accused,
let me assure you, we were obtuse.
To us, men were problems to be
solved & corrected, not the answers
at the back of the book.
                              And how we
loved our books, clutched them
to our cardigans: Keats, Tolstoy,
Thomas Wolfe, Dostoevsky, anyone
with compass or T-square enough
to take the full measure of what
we were: Faust, not Gretchen. Socrates
defining wisdom in the marketplace
not Xanthippe at home pounding out
the phyllo for the baklava. We were told
*The Trojan Women* was man, his suffering,
& we swallowed it, for didn't we too
switch genders for sense & sanity,
laying claim to Ahab's search for truth
in a book of seas, or the phantom itself
hurtling beyond definition?
                              Of those
who held up the mirror showing us
a jumble of geometry, laying us out
in garish polygons & tortured trapezoids—
we argued the merits of modern art,

turned away & paid the price.
                              We wore
our hair-shirts starched & suffered
our virtue gladly. In short, we were afraid.
In love with love, we strained
at the forbidden line. If coerced,
cajoled, or back-seat outmaneuvered,
the next day brought roses, brought *Sorry,*
*it won't happen again.*
                        Was it to our credit,
agreeing to believe the unbelievable?
Were we right to take the high road,
to play the game we couldn't win?
The satin was cut & measured before
we filled our cups, & the only formula
to solve for was the axiom behind the veil:
complement, make the incongruous,
congruous. The threatening acute, right.

# The Rope

FROM PICASSO'S *Boy Leading a Horse*

A naked boy
leads a blue horse
across a desert.
The horse, wild.
The curve of her neck
proclaims it. The boy,
the cork color of the sand,
the horse, a chiaroscuro
of the sky. Each figure
locked in the outline
that summoned it
out of the surrounding
immensity.

The boy faces front
gentling the horse
on a rope that isn't there.
It used to be there. The horse
feels it around her neck.
The boy holds the other end
in his hand. He does not pull.
He loves this filly. She has
a girl's eyes. Her forelock,
her mane, a wash of blue
rising—a dawn color
untouched from the first
pure swath. The boy
has big feet, solid feet.
He knows where he's going.
The horse prances, back hooves
nothing but a blur of joy.
They have been together

a long time, coming
for a long time. When
they find you, they will walk
through the walls of your house
and change everything. You too
may be sacrificed.

# Europa

FROM TITIAN

With a bulging eye, the bull
looks over his shoulder at the girl
he's balancing on his withers. He's
worried he grabbed the wrong one—
she being so joyful about it—this
too healthy girl, legs spread, sprawled
on her back across his bony hump, not
yelling for her mama but lolling
in her draperies as if she were on a divan
expecting company. The time is no time.
The known world of the shore, disappeared.
Read the sky. All that remains is blush.

The girl winds her left hand around
his horn, holding on tenderly, waving
with her right to a platoon of cherubim
who've followed her all the way to this part
of the story so they can tumble from clouds
shooting their little arrows. Later they'll
do their tumbling to decorate another story,
but for now this scene is all there is:
the sea, a wrinkled water, old as the hairy
knees pumping like pistons, whipping it
to a froth to fill the frame. And the rolling
obsidian eye, petrified as an eight-ball
skidding toward a side pocket—big and in trouble.

# Aria for a Green Sky

Before the rain
the swifts go crazy—too many bugs
to eat before night and the last commute
to the chimney.
                Then the storm enters—
low-browed and ruthless—booming itself in
like royalty trailing its marching legions
of rain. Three drenchings a day, the earth
grows tired of it. All those histrionics
to clean up after. And the sodden ground.
                         But the insects
never get tired. They are the milling
chorus crowding the stage, the melodic high
whine of chaos and banquet. *He's coming.*
*He's coming.* El Torero. The Suit of Lights
who winds the wind in his crimson cape.
The Big Man. Breaker of bulls. Prince
of Thunderbolt and perpendicular death.
We clutch our chairs.

Listen to the ghosts bellow
and bang against the narrow stalls of heaven,
the electric fence, the prod. Jammed in
and pawing at the hoof-churned clouds—
red nostrils and wet black hides.

# Apollo Comes to Floyds Knobs, Indiana

Only the lover is *éntheos,* says Plato.
Only the lover is "full of god."
—ROBERTO CALASSO

Everywhere is green—forest green,
moss, jungle, viridian. All Indiana
down to the Ohio, pushing against fences,
swelling with juice. A fat lady
taking up two seats on the airplane.

We used to be forest here
before the urge for acreage and the axe,
pickled beets and church on Sunday.
Forest, before there *was* a Sunday.
Even before God took off for Italy
to have His portrait painted.
And this year, despite what you've
read in the check-out line, the news
isn't who diddled whom sideways,
but that we're being rained on,
flooded, snaked out. Green is in!
*When lilacs last in the dooryard bloom'd?*
Mister, they're eating up the house.

I tell you, Papa's coming home.
He's fed up writing prescriptions
and orders for the medium indifferent.
He's bought himself a bank of clouds,
some killer luggage, and a watering can,
and no kicking the tires or shivering
prayer in a booth is going to stop him.

Before you know it, sycamores will be
sawing through your floorboards. A cedar

big as a myth will rise in your toilet.
And more white pine, Scotch pine, loblolly
than you can count will crash out of your
closets, demanding your furniture back.
With no more TVs, PCs, plug-ins for
your little mouse, who knows what else?
You lose your job. Your son becomes
an English major, and your wife
of thirty-two years decides to throw away
all her clothes and frisk in a laurel tree
naked, insisting she'll not come down
until you learn Greek and climb up,
stripped, hot and hard again with love,
singing *Orea Orea.* Beautiful, beautiful.

*You're kidding,* you say. *My wife,*
*secretary of the bridge club, flashing*
*her puckered thighs and beckoning*
*like the Lorelei, bewitched in varicose*
*and droop?* Mister, just climb up.
Take your belly and bald head and climb
if only because she *is* ridiculous—
an old hen playing chickie on a balcony,
asking only that you rise like the cypress
from your knees and clutch her to you
in all her bravery and redeeming foolishness.
Cradle her face the way you would
a crystal cup you could drink from
forever. Then hurl yourself for once
into your heart's voice. The leaves around
your head will whisper what you need to say.

III

# The Mythological Cod

Soft-finned and waiting,
she feeds under arctic ice
or zigzags down the lacy
edges of Norway. Nereid
of no fat, stretched sleek
up to five, six feet long
cutting through the waters
of the north. *Gadus morhua.*
The Cod. Sensitive eyes,
antifreeze in the blood,
and a cargo of four million
eggs to deliver. A lovesick
bundle of white flakes packed
tight as parachute, tight
as Mae West in a long
green shimmer with amber
leopard spots down the sides,
long white belly and a stripe.
And from her lower jaw, a fleshy
tentacle, a humming dingle-
dangle packed with sensors,
so she'll know you're there.
You warm thing.
                         Just as
Mistress Quickly sensed
the what's what behind
the codpiece—that fancy
bag to hold the bag
Mister Marvelous rides on,
rests on like a pasha. Sack,
reticule, pouch: scrotum.
That pair of maracas,
that holy treasure trove

of Russian dolls.
                    She mates
in spring. The male
bobbing and weaving
then swimming by her side
synchronized to her rhythm
oblivious to nets or a boat's
bottom-cast of shadow, its cage
of lowered strings. How light
the translucent bones in their
flesh of white leaves. How sweet
the rites of urgency, the rush
to release, Oh Oh, together—
tumble of eggs in a baste
of cloudy milt.
                    I remember
Grandma in the cloud
of her dementia, standing by
the stove, rolling codfish balls
for the soup, bending to hear
the kiss of each dropped splash.
And how it occurred to her then
to fess up about Grandpa. *Done.*
*Done as a dead fish.*
                    Battered
by tide and curved as a codpiece,
Cape Cod, named for the fish
that once thrived there, still
lifts an arm, cocks a wrist,
beckons like the Lorelei
to the sea, all the while
hooking like a miser's arm
around treasure. So Captain Gosnold
who named it must have thought,
weighing anchor amid a storm

of Cod—the sacred fish
Christ multiplied to feed
the lucky. A Cod in every pot.
Fish & Chips on Sundays. Enough
to walk on, to pave with scales
the royal road back to England.
A kingdom's purse.
                              A man's purse.
The Stradivarius behind his zipper
or tasseled flap. Rose-tipped
shy or knocking the rhumba
to get out. Broker in a three-
piece suit, standing too close
in the subway, with a fishy stare.
*Wanna ride this deep-sea pole?*
Cod. Imperial in a crown of hair
or ashy pale as my father's
when he died.
                              Enough of that.
Did you know, Cod have
white livers and a vibrating
bone inside the head that
lays down like rings in a tree,
layers to remember? The books say
if you make Cod's head chowder,
better cut away the lips
or put a penny in the pot
for luck, there being other ways
to speak.
                              Once upon a time,
before a place to stand stood
on the face of the deep, the sea,
wrapped in its great sheets
of water, rolled over on its back
and had a dream. And the earth

heaved with it, the sky purpling
with blushing. And all the gods
pacing in their dressing rooms
stopped to polish up their lines.
You know this dream—
how the sea in its soggy sleep
rose, streaming with wet,
knocking the four winds off
their pegs to whizz and bang
against the walls of heaven.
And how Death sank to his knees
and shook in the confines
of his silhouette, for under
the racing eyelids of the sea
swelling as if to break and
singing in the hammock of its aching,
Death saw the dream of the turning wheel.
And hurtling from the teeming depths,
an arc of liquid fire—the Cod.

IV

# Alchemy
BERNHEIM FOREST

In fall the forest turns metallic: gold
fading to copper, falling to quiet,
until all that remains
is the scrape of baser metal—the oak
who denies her leaves but holds on
to give them grief. Her brand
of alchemy: gold into iron, daughters
into a rattling sweater of rusty cans
for the wind to snatch at, swiping
with his hook.
                          Mother, forgive me.
Three years gone, and I'm still
rattling in the shadow of your death.
Tramping these woods, I find myself
looking for substitutes. When I was young
you used to sing to me, but all signs
of a pebble-murmuring brook have dried up.
Roots too—for you were mine surely—
and see how these roots shrivel in air
dangling over a dry culvert. Now
you look back from this forest mirror,
not what you were but what you became.
A stony thing. And there I am, still pushing
your chair, singing "I'm Just Wild about Harry,"
trying to bring you back. That was always
my trouble, wasn't it? Even now, stuck
on my umbilical twig, rattling the dead for a kiss.

# Trip to Delphi

Lately, I've begun to look
like my father. Dead and gone,
the man has sent his genes ahead
to do his dirty work. Baleful eye
in the bathroom mirror, the curse
of the House. And so I've come
not to the holy city of Byzantium
but to the best I can manage—Delphi,
named for the real thing, Indiana,
home of the Wabash and the professional
choice in swine equipment. Delphi,
where girls grow up to be auxiliaries
shuffling behind the fire truck
in the parade.

                     But I remember
the other Delphi—Omphalos of the World—
how twenty years ago I lay on my back
among cypress, the sky opening above me
consenting to be read at last. All columns
up again reaching to touch it. Funny
how the brain works to put things back.
The rubble around me—cracked slabs
and steps where girls once walked
leading the procession, pieces of
pediment and pedestal, each one
white as a Dover Cliff. Oh peerless
dumping ground to hold such trash!
Hunks of marble big as giants' teeth
and strewn about as if the golden cup of
Zeus itself had fallen off its nightstand,
shattering the ineffable bridge.

But what's the bridge between
all that and this Family Dollar store
in Delphi, Indiana, where I've ended up?
This temple consecrated to toothpaste,
batteries, and bargain underwear. Empty
but for me and the thin-lipped guardian of
the till, priestess on a stool, breathing in
the vapors of advanced righteousness. Oh harpy
of the tollgate, agent of the family curse,
do not look at me so. In the twin auguries
of your eyes, double and doubly I am
my father's daughter. Each crumbling face
witness to the other, split in half
and shattered by the bifocal line.

## Far Tar

And who was I
with my New York *cawfee,*
sticking in r's where they're not
or erasing them, as in *Hedder Gablah*
or *Emmer*—guess who—Bovary? So I kept
my face still, not wanting to be impolite
in case I hadn't heard correctly, but then
he said it again—*Far Tar.*

He was talking about its steps
being so slicked with ladybugs,
the rangers had to post KEEP OFF,
so dangerous they were, and what
a shame, because this *Far Tar* was
the forest's most popular attraction.
But by then, not grasping what mystery
he was going on about, I was gone,
slipped down the slide of *Far Tar*
and into the pitch of it. A tar baby
"pitched past pitch of grief," as Hopkins said,
and beyond sense.
                          How far is *Far Tar?*
How many miles of asphalt does it take
to get there? Imagine a road
of good intentions, stretching farther,
further than Dorothy's yellow brick
and tar black to boot. A road of no
return and less traveled by, but not
paved with grief or the sludge of sin
from Dante's fifth *bolgia,* but just
going on and on, zigzagging mountains,
canyons, and herds of wild horses,
then up and down and across the frozen

steppes slippery with history thundering
across the Russias.
                          And what's too
*Far Tar*? Hawthorne's Major Molineux
tarred and feathered beyond recognition.
That's *Far Tar*. Or what about
the British sailor lost to the opium dens
of Shanghai then dumped in the Whangpoo
whose venerable carp still haunt
the spot of his sinking—his last breath,
bubbles clinging to the weeds? So far
from afternoon tea, from Mother
and the playing fields, the mushy peas
of home, and brussels sprouts. I call that
a far Tar. A cold Tar.
                          Coal tar, obtained
from a distillation of bituminous coal,
used for the "heartbreak of psoriasis"
or explosives. Get that stuff over you
and that's *Far Tar*. Or go to North Carolina,
where the Tar River rising in the north
flows a fair and far 215 miles south.
But that's wrong, a misnaming
if there ever was one, for Graves says
*tar* means *west,* Ægean for the dying sun
grateful for a west to crawl into each night
on bloody knees. If so, *Far Tar*
is a synonym for *tar* doubled—*Tartar*.
Not a sauce for fish, but for a west
beyond the West, beyond the beyond
and over the edge, where the grinding gates
of Tartarus open for us all.
                          Who'd have thought

this man manning the desk at the visitor's center
was a historian of such magnitude?
To speak of *Far Tar* and know it
for what it is—Argus-eyed and
foreboding, as if it rose in the midst
of the forest, tall as a fire tower,
to remind us of the long climb
and the steps made slick with ladybugs
who seem more and more like us, forgetting
the fiery house and the smell of children burning.

# The American Heritage

## I. FAITH

Let us speak of the ant. Pismire
in the eye of creation, making extension
ladders of themselves up the broken leg
of the picnic table to reach their reward.
Fat-hungry or sugar, black, brown,
red, or fire, but bustling together
for the common good. Praiseworthy
congregation.
        The book says *Faith*
is belief not resting on logical proof
or material evidence. Here's a story:

Once I watched a lizard watch a wasp
walk across a patio dotted with ants,
her ovipositor swinging beneath her
heavy and bulky as a diaper bag.
She waddled as if she owned the concrete
she walked on. It was *her* downtown,
her shopping mall. She was vulnerable.

The lizard darted out faster than the brain
can register what it thinks it sees—
a dust storm of lightning and blur,
snapped jaws with two wings sticking out,
and a buzz loud as an electric fence,
his tail whipping like a helicopter blade.

When they separated, she stared him down
then went her way. He, ten times bigger
and not knowing how to count to ten,
raged in fury after his own tail before
slinking back behind the flowerpots.
The ants were victorious. Hallelujah!

Spittle on the stem: foam of a nest
and next year's crop of creepy-crawlies
is assured. Silk suspension
swaying from the maple branch—black dot
in the wheel, spinnerets and back legs
securing the trap.
          The book says *Hope*
is the anticipation of what's probable,
expected, sure to swing through that door.
If so, Emily's soul-perching feather duster
has nothing to do with it, and hope is no
*star light star bright* or penny in a well.
Hope is grit your teeth and snare it.
Ask Claudius.
          Or if you prefer your proof
from nature, remember the anteater
who carries his hope around with him—
long and sticky as the state of Florida,
a muscle of flypaper dreaming in his mouth
of the frantic hill.
          Or consider the fruit
of the deadly baneberry, same size, same color
as the poison pearl slipped into the cup.
Each launched in hope. The telling difference is
nature is prolific, producing ten, twenty
on a stem. Man, bless him, is more hopeful.
Claudius needed only one.

How do you measure charity?
An orange in a sock? A trussed-up turkey
left on a porch? A check written with an eye
for tax purposes?
                    The book says *Charity*
is the provision of help or relief to the poor,
the original *Caritas* cleaned up to *Agape*—
St. Paul's notion of love. But what did Paul
know about charity or love? *Caritas* meant Grace,
not God's but the Grace of the primordial Goddess,
and about *that* kind of charity, it was Mother
who could have taught him a thing or two.

She kept it on a hook in her closet,
back behind the dresses. Your hand would
have to know where it was to find it. So deep
the shadows of that labyrinth and the forbidden
closet door she undressed behind.
                                    It happened
on nights I'd hear my father cry, a grown man
sobbing on the rack of his cuckoldry, and I
who knew nothing yet about love's deception
*or* charity, knew enough to keep to my room
and not venture out until well after
I heard the clack of hangers being pushed aside—
her arm groping in the dark for the closet's red
rubbery heart, its black nozzle with the funny tip.

# Reverie

### 1

November's deluge
plasters the leaves to the ground
in layers, wetting them down
for pliability then for packing.
Making room.
                            All last week's crisp flying—
those plucky gliders—wet as wet
laundry now, tired as refugees.

The earth will take them all.
There's *always* room at that inn.

Autumn after autumn.
Funny how one never gets tired, pressed
to the window, watching, the way
you would a favorite movie. Gene Kelly
still singing in the rain.

### 2

Singing in the rain,
autumn is alto. And didn't Shelley
say the same? A woman of a certain age, wide
and golden at the girth, who each year
emerges from the green screens of summer
to show us her dress before
allowing the wind to take it, little
by little, off.
                            Today she's wearing
my Japanese maple. A red glory
lifting a thousand kisses to the rain. A silk
kimono so loosely tied, you can almost hear
her singing as it slides off.

Listen—
a cello hums in the heartwood, your mother
or mine, moaning on death's baronial bed.


3

Moaning? I hear no moaning. Today's
rain keeps me inside, deaf by window
and blurry blinded. What a relief.

Rilke's *scenery of departure*
too bright this year. The gorgeousness too
gem-cut, too desperate, flooding the eye
with news too piercing to bear. Each tree
a four-alarm fire quivering for
attention. *How all occasions do*
*inform against me.* Just when I think

I can take no more, there's another
shrug off a stem, a last little sour
grape before the letting go. Last chance
to deliver, going, going, gone.

# In the Summer of Cathedrals and Titian Reds

I am studying my iconography,
while Bruce, rumpled as a paper bag,
sleeps through the conductor's rounds.
And except for two girls from Düsseldorf
killing the miles to Rome over Yahtzee,
no two people look together at the same thing,
not in here or outside this train window
where Leonardo's wind-whipped hills rise
spattered with the blood of poppies
stuck in their stories, babbling in tongues.

If in a cart she's carting around
her spiked and bloody wheel, you know
it's Saint Catherine. Holy Sebastian
if he's tied to a post, quivering in arrows—
the human pincushion. Pale Agatha—
Lamb of God—if she's serving up her breasts,
cut off and cute as two gelati on a plate,
her eyes heavenward, piteous and drowned.

How persistent these saints
groaning in the oils of their burning,
driven to show & tell their page
in the church bulletin—skinned, crushed,
raked by carding combs, roasted alive.
Hooked by martyrdom, each one surrendered,
knowing it would take that running on the knife
pleading, *Look at me Look at me.* That much.

So imagine, in this summer of saints
and second-class compartments, the mystery
when my lunch tomato squirts, splat
on a stranger's newly pressed pants—blood

splotch and sacrifice, John the Baptist's
gusher of spurting neck. And I, doomed
and typecast by the fact of it, find myself
up and twirling in my last clean T-shirt, belly

bumping the good news to the blind:
Look. There's this bakery in Sorrento—
morning rolls hot-tucked with olives
and prosciutto. The nectar of blood oranges
in Agrigento. And a proprietor in Firenze
on the Via dell'Angelo who knows how to place
a swirl on a cappuccino in the sign of the nebula,
the mystic spiral, seal and covenant—cinnamon sweet
as the whorl in the ear of God or the seventh veil
dropped lightly on the froth of heaven.

## Modigliani's Girls

It isn't their faces
that draw us in, but his outlines
straining to hold them, for who'd buy beauty
without a cage to put it in. Think *escape*
and half the world burns down.

But who is this, face tipped
to one side and the coppery hair—
the outline delicate as an exploring finger.
*Toujours amour* or one more
plucked flower too heavy for her neck?
Why else would he twist her mouth like that,
paint her eyes pupil-less and all green iris:
two upholstery tacks pinning her down.

Still, how could he let that flesh tone
go—Jeanne Hébuterne, the tawny slip
of low sun that lit up his rooms.
Another doomed Puccini girl driven
to gather up her skirts and her eight-month
pregnancy, and at twenty-one years old
walk backwards through a fifth-floor window.
No outline to hold her now that the hand
that painted it lay white and slack on the sheets.

You can almost hear the music.

# The Shoes

This poem is about a bed and a chair,
about a pair of shoes, and a body
I knew better than my own, the husband's
body my body has forgot. Nor would
I recognize or recall—if it walked
in now in those shoes I picked out for him—
the old hollows, the way our flesh must have
waked and curved to each other, how sinews
of his shoulder were attached to carve out
the place I lay my head.
                                   This is about
what happens to what you can't remember
because the mind's job is to save your life—
cauterizing, cutting it out. What's gone
is forced to wander the brain looking for
the warm spot, the open-arms spot where it
used to live. Only things remain—a chair,
a pair of empty shoes scurrying down
the neural corridors, scuffing up dust,
dropping echoes like desperate pebbles in
their wake, having nothing but a voiceless
tongue of dried leather, all frenzy and wag.

# The Color of Ineffable

Yesterday on my walk, a Polyphemus moth,
dead. All color drained
but for the great dark eyes on her wings.
How could I not bring her home? She was
bleached perfection, the color of faded silk
or a brittle papyrus on which were written
the now unreadable inks and the cocoon's mystery.

The expert says she died of starvation,
having used up all the fat
from her salad days. But he can't explain
her lack of color or why she appeared
in the one spot between sunshine and shade
where I'd be sure to find her.

I keep her on the corner of my desk,
marvel at her six-inch spread, the night-
flying veins bursting like moon rays
from the center post of her body—a wonder,
a week's worth of wonder, for seven days
is all she had. So says Professor Moth,
and he must know. But I like to think
when her allotted time was up,
she in her hour of certitude put aside
all purples and gold, all buzz of sequin
and flutter and whim, and like a queen
facing the wall of inevitable,
laid the white flag of herself down naked:
elect: the devil's parchment, the angel's chalk.

The professor says impossible.
But what does he know about epic queens
or poets in white? And what could he understand
about women and starve?

# Leonardo's Roses

FROM *Lady with an Ermine*
CZARTORYSKI MUSEUM, KRAKOW

Leonardo was convinced
sperm came down from the brain
through a channel in the spine.
So much for genius. I say
sperm, like any seed, travels up,
makes an explosion in the brain
leaving a scent of crushed flowers
in the memory. On such a trellis
true love might climb. On such
a shaky stair, many a bad apple
rotten to the core is persuaded
to polish himself up before rising,
sleek and feverish as a column
of mercury in a tube.
                    Mona Lisa
whose smile is older than the rocks,
she knew. And Cecilia Gallerani,
seventeen and paramour to Sforza
the lecher, usurper, Duke of Milan.
See how she catches the light
full in the face then beams it back
like truth itself. And look
how she holds the ermine—
Sforza's emblem—how she lets it
tread her arm, claws unleashed,
and she not flinching. This is
no inert female sitting pretty
for her picture.
                    She's present,
expectant, listening to someone
over Leonardo's hunched shoulder,
maybe Sforza himself who follows

her scent up and down corridors
in case he needs her, yes,
to check his arithmetic, polish up
his correspondence. Later when
he's pricked to marry someone else,
he'll set her up for life: estate,
gardens, the works. *Cecilia Magnificat.*
But she doesn't know that yet, does she—
stroking his little white weasel,
patting its head?

V

# Working in Metal

BERNHEIM FOREST

Today's forest floor, a terrazzo
of copper leaf. The remaining scrub
also copper: copper breath, penny
breath, too faint to call it rustling.
The mother trees of summer—
those iron lungs—streamed oxygen
from paps that swayed sweet
rock-a-byes in green blouses. But now
all is brittle air. Underfoot snap and crack.
And all crowns, by necessity, forget
what lies shriveling at their feet.

What's imperishable is perishable
piece by piece. The soaking rains,
the split and suffering bark, the sink-
hole in the dirt assures it: green to gold
to copper to fade. Here is not Florida. Here
winter's point is blunt. Juice and fondle
give way to December's iron chop,
and the forest lives because it dies.
How's that for conundrum?

But now, there is only now
and this walking. My fingers, numb.
My breath, a magician's string of scarves,
or my own good ghost rehearsing
how to vacate her chilly rental. Five o'clock
and the air tastes of pewter. Tonight
the sky will contract, tightening in a thin-
lipped grudge until it cannot help
but ease itself down, giggling in white
and whimsy. And once more

before I quit this place, I will scarf and
boot and bundle up, to greet the mothers
shawled in white wool, and leave my prints
in the buried patches of copper made soft
by such fine soaking. Intaglio. Art to last.

# Birches

FROM CHEKHOV

What is paradise without longing?
Yesterday outside my window
four deer. This morning, a brilliant sun
splashing down a merriment of leaves.
All week, blessings and blue skies. And I
am Masha or Olga or a young Irina
yanked out of the sleep perfection put me in,
saying Moscow. Let's all pack up and go to Moscow.

The samovar hums, a cup rattles the saucer.
Whose hands are shaking? Look,
deer step out delicately, birds flap south,
and here we are imitating birch trees—
long white faces and mournful eyes. Remember
how Grandmother used to butter her bread
on both sides? What's not possible?

Get out the chocolates, Father's silver
letter opener, raspberry jam for the tea.
Load them up. Wrap the corsets and camisoles
in tissue paper, and don't forget pastels
in case it rains, and my good black dress
for afternoon charades. Where's the leash?
Where's my parasol? Perhaps in Moscow
I shall play lady with a dog and fall in love.
Stop giggling. Where are Mother's opera glasses?
We'll need them, hat pins too, and, oh yes,
galoshes. Remember the galoshes.

What did you say about the birches
seeming so pained to watch our going?
Well then, we'll take them too, replant them

in gaily painted pots up and down
Petrovsky Boulevard. Clap your hands.
Call for the carriage. Are we really going?

Who said that? Surely it's written
there's time enough before the curtain
to tie up our bonnets and board the train.
Already the servants are waving handkerchiefs,
wiping their eyes like extras in a play.
Look at them, such pinched faces.
If I didn't know better, I'd say they're calculating
just how long it will take for us to come back.

## Medea

I walk through the year's final dapple,
that slow rollover of sun to shade to
bright again. The woods are still, the trees
concentrating on upright: weightlifters
holding up their last tons of rustling.
And I see how the forest empties
from the bottom up, saving the youngest—
that burst at the top—for last.

I think of my family, that high-
strung whine of guilt and blame,
that staircase always threatening
down, and the terrible politeness
of lock the door and don't speak of it,
and I wonder the mutation of genes
to go against a nature that seed-covers
its children: husks, wings, keys, pods—
the infinite variety to protect, provide.

In the midst of the forest, an abandoned theater
of mossy stones waits for the next performance.
Around it, wild birch remembering the last one.
The eyes in their trunks still frozen open.

## Art & Science

In chemistry, what's severed
looks to latch on to any other
severed thing: orphaned electrons
zizzing in your wires race to embrace,
swirl a DC-do-ing, re-form their rings.
Chemistry likes adherence, every tick
its tock. Split an atom. What a noise!

Then is it not passing strange
when molecules into proteins make
and muster into muscle, teeth, bone, knee,
that when this vast multitude jostling
under skin wakes, it wants to be alone?

What did Greta Garbo have on me?

Outside my window the great poplar
tosses her leaves hand to hand like
so much change as if she were rooted
to a corner waiting for a bus. How antsy
she is for all this autumn fuss to be over.
Who knows but that November rains
whet the appetite for cold: the annual
jettison of gold to stripped-down shudder
and pause. The air holds its breath. Listen.
One red dot on a bare branch, singing.
In here, the violin's one note at a time.

# Talking to The Eternal Light

I recall a tree. A road
close by for parking, but no
marble wall to my left
nor could there have been time
in these intervening years
to build one. The surrounding
lawns were empty. Virginal.
No muddy-mouthed crowd
jostling under grass. No, this
is not the place. Don't look at
me like that. It's not my memory
that's broken. Two rows of chairs,
a green awning, the rabbi's hired
platitudes, the pink lipstick
she wouldn't have been caught dead in,
she was caught dead in. See?
I remember. And I tell you, here
is not where I put her down. Or him.
I don't care how long you've been
in business (your eye's twitching).
Maybe they moved themselves,
tunneling to a final destination:
the bronze marker—heavy
as their conjugal headache—
pulled across lawns, so attached
to its underground team of galloping
boxes, it hung on like Ahab
clinging to the rope of his phantom.
That's how you read me, isn't it?
Hanging on and desperate, the way
a lost child sure he sees his parents ahead,
runs, crying out to reach them before
they—eyes now only for each other—
turn that corner and disappear.

# Getting Serious

Today I started looking for my soul.
Yesterday it was my keys. Last week,
my brain which I couldn't find, it being out
looking for me, now that I'm getting so old.

First I thought my soul would have gone
back to Greece where she grew so tall and straight,
she thought she was a column. Or back to camp,
being forever twelve and underdeveloped.
Perhaps, being careless, I left her during the 70s
in bed with God knows whom. Or could be
I buried her with my mother—my head not being right—
but that was my heart.

So I went to where I know
I saw her last. Radio City Music Hall.
I'm six, my feet barely brushing the floor,
and the Rockettes start shuffling out, long-
legged and perfect as paper dolls kicking up
down in a wave. One body with seventy-two knees
chugging like pistons going back in a forever mirror,
same as in Coney Island's Fun House or on Mama's can
of Dutch Cleanser. And my heart flexed in me, a sail,
and I swear I saw it flying out of my chest
spiriting away my giddy soul, ears plugged and tied
to the mast: *I can't hear you I can't hear you.*

# Genealogy

Yesterday, Kafka's grave. Today,
the old Jewish quarter, cobblestones,
little shops huddled in alleys. Then,
the old cemetery where for five hundred
years, Jews were buried standing up,
space being denied them. You know—
*no room at the inn,* that old line.
Imagine—shoulder to shoulder, twelve
to a grave, the ranks closing in
close and deep with not a sound
to give away their position. Twelve mutes
face front in a stuck elevator, phalanx
of the well-behaved.

                  Then lunch—blinis
and borscht with sour cream and potatoes,
the latest discovery of my too-young husband,
cookie of my age, who tends to tender me
too careful, the way you would a Belgian lace
or any sad curiosity. *You okay?* he asks
then checks the authenticity of my reply
as if checking my temperature,
for we are off to the Pinkas Synagogue
with its lists of the Holocaust dead—
room after room, ceiling to floor,
you'd think the walls would collapse,
there are so many.

                  And I wonder
what he's *really* looking for, my sweet Protestant
to whom religion means pitch-in suppers
and learning to be nice. And who am I
to be treasured so, but the one link he has
to Christendom's black hole and this long

chain of names, not of the merely dead,
but of the double dead, the corpseless, visit-
less dead whose names remain the only things left
to teeter on the edge of abstraction.

What enduring hurt still knocking for redress
awoke in him today that makes him bend
to this wall in a borrowed yarmulke,
too blue-eyed, too white-sneakered American,
combing through these endless lists of names? So intent,
you'd think he was looking for his own.

# The Waiting Room

To speak of crucial
in a life of the merely interesting,
to have a yen for it, a calling you might say,
is to be perpetually involved
in the act of naming. And yet, when I went
to the one place where crucial happened
not once but over and over again,
I gagged on my own silence.

There is ash at Birkenau
under your every step. It hisses in the long
uncut grasses growing out of its mouths.
Nothing but this sibilance is left, this ocean
of wind-tortured tongues. The air
not big enough to hold it.

Never mind sixty years of museums
and memorials, vigils and eternal lights.
Never mind that everything to be said
has been said. I needed to translate.
The singed grass demanded it.

Birkenau means Place of Birches—
the grove in the meadow next to which
Crematorium IV was built and fired up to run
twenty-four hours a day, so busy gassing
and burning there'd be a back-up
waiting to go in.

Imagine the humiliations of the flesh
fumbling to cover up in that waiting room
of white trees, those totems of eyes. Imagine
your mother, her sparse patch. The unopened

pink purse that is your daughter. Then now,
with the wind up and the whipping grasses
wild at your knees, before the dogs come,
*hurry* write the choke of terror.

# The Iron Cross

BERNHEIM FOREST

Three-leafed, I figured it was a kind
of shamrock, but red, the color of old slaughter.
I thought of romantic Ireland dead and gone,
Maud Gonne in her grave and Yeats's tree
watered by sacrifice and blood. But when
I discovered its name, I heard jackboots
and the Panzer Division grinding over Europe
and imagined another kind of bleeding, the ground
still sickened with it. I walked away.

Past the river birches and the tupelos,
past the tamarack in its copse of cousins,
then up to the overlook and bench
dedicated to Rebecca Ruth Gutgsell
who lived forty-four years on this earth
and in whose memory I sit among twenty-three
Virginia pines, tall and thin and rich
with cones. And I wonder, because
for Rebecca (and me) those Iron Crosses
cross too close for comfort, if sitting here
she'd notice how the pine's bark looks crack-
toothed, the color of clot or bleeding brick,
and conclude that these trees too
were placed in memory, but for a whole city
ground under a boot, pulverized by war.

I know, I am prone to projection,
but a world beyond my say-so and how
is too inconceivable a place to live. Once I saw
an Australian eucalyptus that oozed red
at the slightest scrape, and I remember thinking,
*Here stands Mother caught in some vegetable dream*

*of suffering—her favorite halo.* Or the time
at Birkenau when the grasses, grown long and
sleek from the ash that fed them, hissed at my knees.

Iron Crosses. Yesterday I went back.
They had sprouted flowers, baby pinks
laundered clean as Hawthorne's ribbons. But the leaves—
so frail to suggest such purpose—shimmying
in the light wind, you'd swear they were laughing.

# Design

As of last inspection, all my ghosts
are present and accounted for
and, it appears, happy
as if the terrible airlessness
agreed with them. When I ache to connect
they seem amused at my foolishness,
stuck as I am in the old game of breathing.

Time is the culprit, flapping about me,
demanding to be used. While they,
on the other side of that door,
have traveled far beyond
the stopped watch dangling off the bone.

They ride a bigger clock. Earth's
round and around, pony on a track.
The Jurassic, washed away
by the Cretaceous, the Miocene
by the Pliocene. Each age, each century,
sloshed off in the grand soak and swirl
of spinning cycles. While I, peering out
the narrow windows of my sight,
know only one year at a time: one more
ragged spring hosed down and drained away.

Oh House of Shining Windows that is the sky,
of course they are happy. The stuff
that was Mama, soldier of scour and rag,
made Queen in the royal army of clean-up.
While the pit bull that was my father,
runs, vindicated at last, snarling,
nipping at the heels of thunder, pulling down rain.

POSTLUDE

## On Deck

April in Georgia and the dogwood
droops peevish. Ten in the morning,
95 in the shade, and the pond—
where a friend swears he once saw
a beaver slap his tail—gags on mud.

But weather or not, new shoots
of kudzu inching across the ground
look for a sapling to mount, while
birds, as if demented, keep up
their eggy songs of love. Funny
how wooing goes on no matter what.
Or where. Just yesterday, never
mind the UV rays taking advantage
of peepholes in the ozone, we walked
our flesh outside—me with my droop
and advancing state of crepiness, and he,
formerly known as *sweet young thing,*
bifocaled now and balding. Think old—
Adam and his girl come home
lugging their baggage and their deaths
but still hand-in-hand courageous
despite their once-upon-a-time bitter
dish of apple crumble, only to face
on their return to nakedness
the white oak's shudder and groan,
the April poplar turning away its leaves.
Damn sun suckers! Little Puritans!

Maybe in November, when light's
absence squeezes the day from both ends
and all last-ditch efforts of October's
in-your-face glitterings are flattened underfoot,

those leaves will look back, not on their spring
but on their final frippery, and what smug
joy it was. That defiance. That withering *HA!*

# NOTES

"Seeing It Through." This poem is in answer to Louise Glück's poem "Birthday," wherein she expresses amazement at reaching the age of fifty.

"Imitating Nature." Information on the ancient Egyptian treatment of breasts can be found in "Blue," in *The Primary Colors: Three Essays*, by Alexander Theroux.

"Europa." The Titian painting referred to is *The Rape of Europa*, which is in the Isabella Stewart Gardner Museum in Boston.

"The Mythological Cod." The title and idea came from my husband's fortunate misreading of my son-in-law's entry while playing the game "Dictionary." Much of the scientific and historical information comes from the book *Cod*, by Mark Kurlansky.

"Far Tar." The quotation from Gerard Manley Hopkins is from his sonnet 42. The information about the Ægean meaning of *tar* is from *The White Goddess*, by Robert Graves.

"*The American Heritage*." The information about *caritas*, the original meaning of "charity," comes from *The Woman's Encyclopedia of Myths and Secrets*, by Barbara G. Walker.

"Leonardo's Roses." The information about da Vinci's thoughts on the origin of sperm was found at the Papyrus Museum, Vienna, Austria.

# ACKNOWLEDGMENTS

I wish to thank the editors of the following journals, in which these poems first appeared:

*Boulevard:* "Apollo Comes to Floyds Knobs, Indiana" and "Imitating Nature"

*Chattahoochee Review:* "*The American Heritage*"

*Ekphrasis:* "Leonardo's Roses"

*Field:* "Alchemy"

*Florida Review:* "Europa"

*Georgia Review:* "Aria for a Green Sky," "Autobiography: The Short Version," "In the Summer of Cathedrals and Titian Reds," "On Deck," "Silent Movie," and "Vinculum"

*Gettysburg Review:* "The Black Tupelo," "The Color of Ineffable," "Far Tar," "The Iron Cross," "The Price," "Reverie," "Visiting the Territories," "Waiting," and "Watching You in the Mirror" (as "Teeth")

*Image:* "Working in Metal"

*Indiana Review:* "Genealogy"

*New Letters:* "Geometry"

*New Millennium Writings:* "Cascade Falls"

*Ploughshares:* "Getting Serious"

*Poetry:* "Art & Science," "Permanent Press," "Seeing It Through," and "Trip to Delphi"

*Shenandoah:* "Birches," "Design," "The Rope," "The Shoes," and "Wind"

*Southern Poetry Review:* "*Medea*"

*Southern Review:* "The Mythological Cod," "Siren Song for Late September," and "The Waiting Room"

"*Ars Poetica* in Green" is reprinted from *Prairie Schooner,* vol. 73, no. 2 (Summer 1999), by permission of the University of Nebraska Press. Copyright 1999 by the University of Nebraska Press.

"Talking to The Eternal Light" is reprinted from *Prairie Schooner,* vol. 81, no. 4 (Winter 2007), by permission of the University of Nebraska Press. Copyright 2007 by the University of Nebraska Press.

"Depression Glass" and "Modigliani's Girls" are reprinted from *Prairie Schooner,* vol. 82, no. 3 (Fall 2008), by permission of the University of Nebraska Press. Copyright 2008 by the University of Nebraska Press.

Some of these poems have been anthologized in the following publications: *Alhambra Poetry Calendar, 2008,* ed. Shafiq Naz; *The Best American Poetry, 2009,* ed. David Wagoner (Scribner, 2009); *Blood to Remember: American Poets on the Holocaust,* rev. 2nd ed., ed. Charles Ades Fishman (Time Being Books, 2007); *Cadence of Hooves: A Celebration of Horses,* ed. Suzan Jantz (Yarroway Mountain Press, 2008); *Celebrating Seventy,* ed. Jenny Kander (Wind Publications, 2003); *Love Over 60: An Anthology of Women's Poems,* ed. Robin Chapman and Jeri McCormick (Mayapple Press, 2010); *Red, White, and Blues: Poets on the Promise of America,* ed. Virgil Suárez and Ryan G. Van Cleave (University of Iowa Press, 2004); *When She Named Fire: An Anthology of Contemporary Poetry by American Women,* ed. Andrea Hollander Budy (Autumn House, 2009). Several poems have also been featured online in the *Innisfree Poetry Journal* 9 (2009).

I am grateful to the I. W. Bernheim Foundation for the 2003–04 Writing Fellowship at Bernheim Forest and Arboretum—particularly LaDonna Eastman, Julie Schweitzer, Bill Hiser, and all the research staff who were more than helpful—for many glorious weeks of poems and trees. I also wish to thank the Mary Anderson Center for the Arts, the MacDowell Colony, the *Georgia Review/*

Bowers House Literary Center, and the Carson McCullers Center for Writers and Musicians, where many of these poems were written. Most especially, a heartfelt thank-you to Laura Newbern and Andrea Hollander Budy for their insights and invaluable help in organizing the manuscript. To Dale Kushner—friend in song and sister in the struggle—this book could not have been written without you.